FRETBOARD ROADMAPS DOBRO™ GUITAR

THE ESSENTIAL GUITAR PATTERNS THAT ALL THE PROS KNOW AND USE

BY FRED SOKOLOW

PLAYBACK+
Speed • Pitch • Balance • Loop

To access audio, visit:
www.halleonard.com/mylibrary

4660-2345-1195-2316

The Recording

Guitar and Vocals—Fred Sokolow
Sound Engineer and Other Instruments—Dennis O'Hanlon
Recorded at O'Hanlon Recording and Music Services

ISBN 978-0-634-00141-3

HAL•LEONARD®

Visit Hal Leonard Online at **www.halleonard.com**

Explore the entire family of Hal Leonard products and resources

World headquarters, contact:
Hal Leonard
7777 West Bluemound Road
Milwaukee, WI 53213
Email: info@halleonard.com

In Europe, contact:
Hal Leonard Europe Limited
Dettingen Way
Bury St Edmunds, Suffolk, IP33 3YB
Email: info@halleonardeurope.com

In Australia, contact:
Hal Leonard Australia Pty. Ltd.
4 Lentara Court
Cheltenham, Victoria, 3192 Australia
Email: info@halleonard.com.au

CONTENTS

INTRODUCTION

Dobro (acoustic lap-style slide guitar) is often heard in country music and bluegrass, and its electric cousin, lap steel, is associated with traditional country music, Hawaiian music, and Western swing. But acoustic and electric lap-slide (steel) guitar also sound great in blues, rock, swing and jazz. Accomplished steel guitarists can play all these styles. They can ad lib solos and play backup in any key—all over the fretboard, and they can play in several open tunings.

There are moveable patterns on the guitar fretboard that make it easy to do these things. The pros are aware of these "fretboard roadmaps," even if they don't read music. If you want to play electric or acoustic lap-slide with other people, this is essential guitar knowledge.

You need the fretboard roadmaps if...

▶ All your steel soloing sounds the same and you want variety in your playing.

▶ Some keys are harder to play in than others.

▶ You can't automatically play any steel lick you can think or hum.

▶ You know a lot of steel guitar "bits and pieces," but you don't have a system that ties it all together.

Read on, and many mysteries will be explained. Since you're serious about playing steel guitar, the pages that follow can shed light and save you a great deal of time.

Good luck,

Fred Sokolow

This book is a steel guitarist's extension of Fred Sokolow's *Fretboard Roadmaps* (Hal Leonard, HL00696514), which includes even more music theory for guitarists, along with musical examples, solos and licks. We urge you to use *Fretboard Roadmaps* as a reference, along with this book. Also consult Fred Sokolow's *Roots of Slide Guitar*, published by Hal Leonard.

THE RECORDING AND THE PRACTICE TRACKS

All the licks, riffs and tunes in this book are played on the accompanying recording.

There are also four Practice Tracks on the recording. Each track illustrates a specific soloing style, such as "first position steel licks in open G tuning," or "steel in standard tuning in the key of E." They are mixed with the steel guitar on one side of your stereo and the backup band on the other, so you can tune out the steel guitar and practice playing solos with the backup band.

To access the audio files, go to **www.halleonard.com/mylibrary** and enter the code found on page 1.

PRELIMINARIES

In lap-style guitar, all notes are fretted with the steel instead of with the fingers.

USING A STEEL

► Hold the steel with your thumb, index and middle fingers, as shown below.

► Rest your little finger and ring finger on the strings *behind the steel,* to eliminate unwanted noises.

► Fret the strings *lightly* with the steel; don't try to press the strings down to the fretboard.

► Hold the steel *right over the fretwires,* not between them. Otherwise, your notes will be flat or sharp.

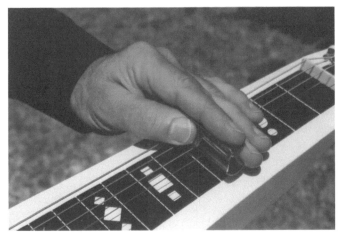

How To Hold The Steel

Steel for lap steel player   **"Stevens steel," preferred by Dobro players**

SEVERAL WAYS TO SLIDE

► You can slide up to a note from a few frets back.

► You can slide down from a note.

► You can slide back and forth between notes.

► You can play notes without sliding, using your ring and little fingers to damp the strings.

► You can emphasize or sustain a note by shaking your left hand from the wrist while fretting a string. This gives you a singing *vibrato.*

All these techniques are illustrated in the following exercise, which is played in G tuning (see **ROADMAP #1**):

1 To access this track and others, go to **www.halleonard.com/mylibrary** and enter the code found on page 1.

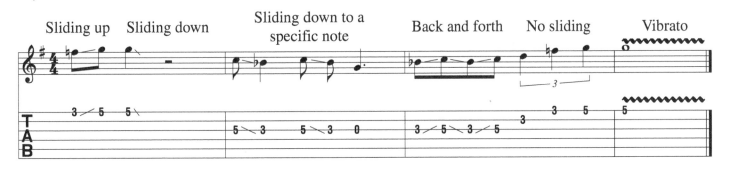

FINGERPICKS

Many lap steel and Dobro players use a thumbpick (usually plastic) and two metal fingerpicks. They fit on your picking hand as shown in the picture below:

Fingerpicks

G TUNING: FIRST POSITION

Blues Scale

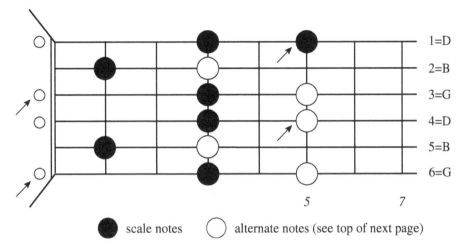

1=D
2=B
3=G
4=D
5=B
6=G

5   7

● scale notes   ○ alternate notes (see top of next page)

Major Scale

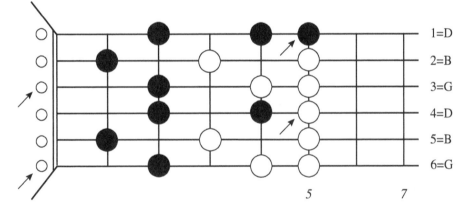

1=D
2=B
3=G
4=D
5=B
6=G

5   7

WHY?

▶ Very similar to the Mississippi Delta G tuning used by blues players, this G tuning is useful in all kinds of music. Once you're familiar with the above scales, you can play countless melodies and licks in first position, in "open G" tuning.

WHAT?

▶ *Both of the above diagrams are for G tuning.* When you strum the open (unfretted) strings in this tuning, you play a G major chord. That's why it's often called "open G tuning."

▶ *The major scale is the "do-re-mi" eight-note scale on which so much music is based. The blues scale is pentatonic* (it consists of five notes). The flatted third and seventh are sometimes called "blue notes."

▶ *The scales are guidelines.* Sometimes other notes (between the notes indicated above) work.

▶ *The arrows point out the tonic (G) notes,* also called root notes. Notice the high tonic note at the 5th fret. A lot of licks will resolve on this note, or on other G notes.

► *The white dots (circles that are not filled in) are "alternates."* They are duplicated by open strings or by higher strings. For example, the 4th string/5th fret and the open 3rd string are both G. The 6th string/5th fret and the 5th string/1st fret are both C.

HOW?

► *To get to G tuning from standard tuning:*
The 4th (D), 3rd (G) and 2nd (B) strings stay as they are in standard tuning.
Tune the 6th/E string up three frets, to G. Match it to the open 3rd string.
Tune the 5th/A string up two frets, to B. Match it to the open 2nd string.
Tune the 1st/E string down two frets, to D. Match it to the 2nd string/3rd fret.

► *Play the scales ascending and descending, starting from a G note.*

Blues Scale G Tuning

Major Scale

► *Use the "alternate notes" for sliding or vibrato.* You can't slide to an open 3rd string/G note, but you can slide up to the same G note at the 4th string/5th fret. You can't play vibrato at the open 1st string/D, but you can play vibrato on the same D note at the 2nd string/3rd fret.

DO IT!

► *Use the blues scale to ad-lib solos throughout a bluesy tune.* In spite of the chord changes in "Rocky Blues," all the soloing is based on the G blues scale.

Rocky Blues

G Tuning

8

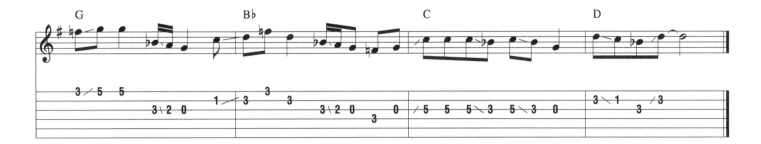

▶ *Use the blues scale to play melodies and blues licks.* In the following solo, the guitar plays the melody to the old blues, "See, See Rider," including ad-lib blues licks that fill the pauses between melodic phrases.

See, See Rider

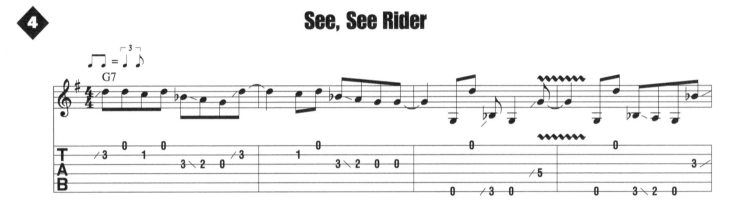

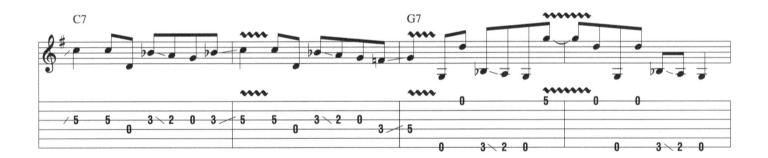

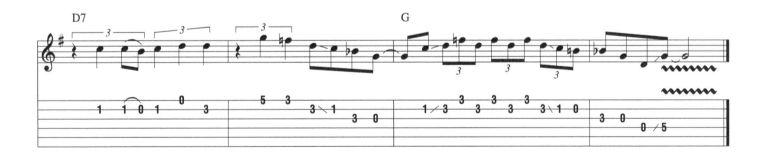

▶ Use the major scale to play melodies and ad lib solos. In "Chilly Winds," following, the melody and fills are based on the major scale.

Chilly Winds

G Tuning

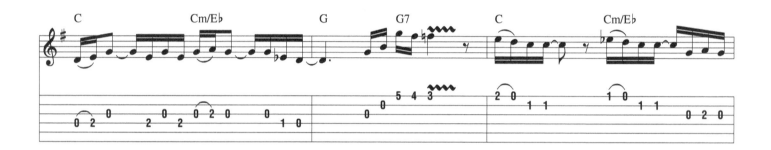

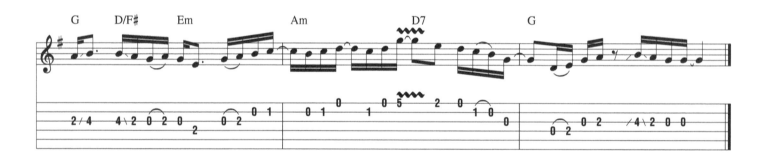

SUMMING UP — NOW YOU KNOW...

▶ How to play a first-position G blues scale

▶ How to play a first-position G major scale

▶ How to use both scales to play melodies and ad lib solos and licks

2

G Blues Scale

G Major Scale

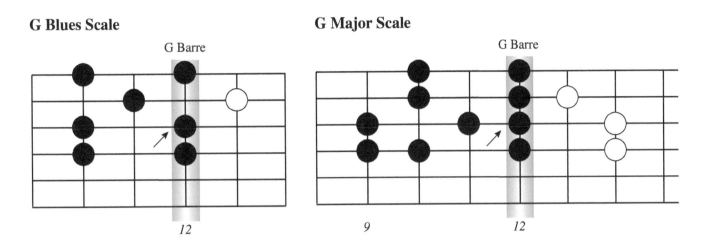

WHY?

▶ The scales in **ROADMAP #2** make it possible to solo and ad lib licks in any key.

WHAT?

▶ *The above diagrams show two moveable scales: G major and G blues.* Both scales have the same "home base": the barred G chord at the 12th fret. The arrows point out the tonic (G) notes.

▶ *The scales are "moveable" because they use no open strings.* If you play the G major scale two frets lower (using the barred F chord at the 10th fret for a home base), it's an F major scale.

▶ *The white dots are "alternates."* They are duplicated by lower notes. For example, the 4th string/14th fret and the 3rd string/9th fret are both E.

HOW?

▶ *Play the scales ascending and descending, starting from a G note:*

G Tuning

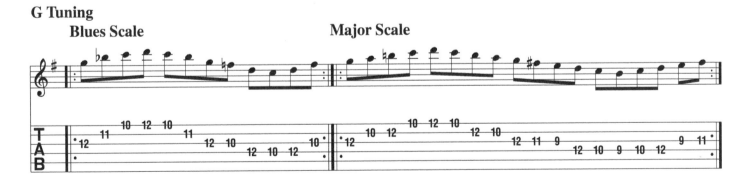

► *Play both moveable scales in other keys.* For example, a barre at the 10th fret is an F chord. Play an F blues scale and F major scale:

F Blues Scale

F Major Scale

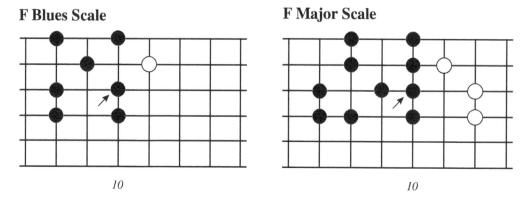

10   *10*

DO IT!

► *Use the moveable blues scale to ad lib solos to bluesy tunes* like "Rocky Blues," from **ROADMAP #1**.

6

Rocky Blues II (at 12th Fret)

G Tuning

► *Use the moveable blues scale to play bluesy melodies and licks in keys other than G.* "See, See Rider II," which follows, is in the key of E (at the 9th fret):

7

See, See Rider II (Key of E)

G Tuning

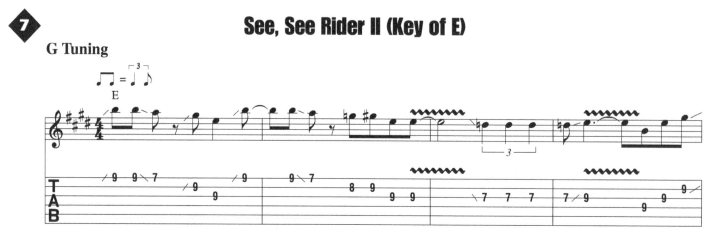

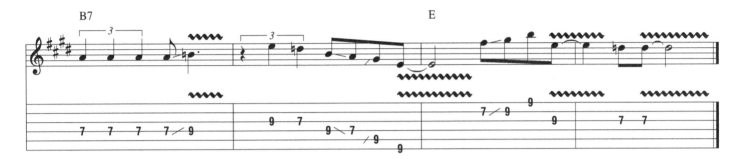

► *Use the moveable major scale to play melodies and solos.* Here's a melodic solo to "Amazing Grace" in the key of F (10th fret):

8

Amazing Grace

G Tuning

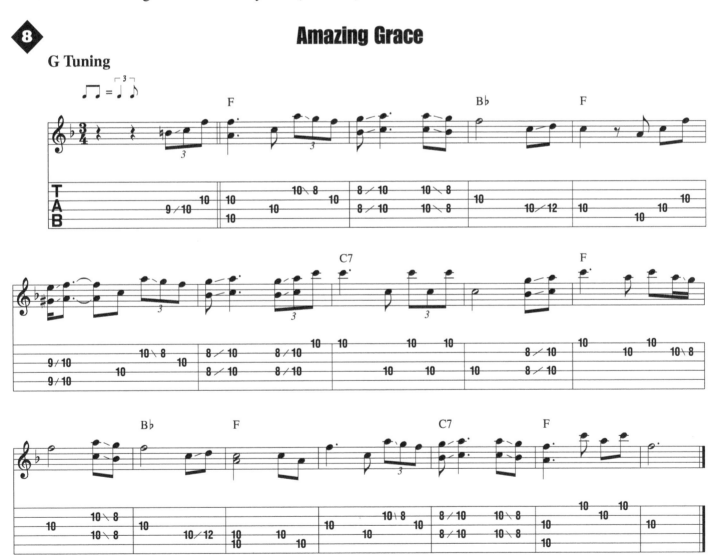

▶ *Use the moveable major scale to ad lib backup licks to "Red River Valley,"* in the key of C (5th fret):

Red River Valley

G Tuning

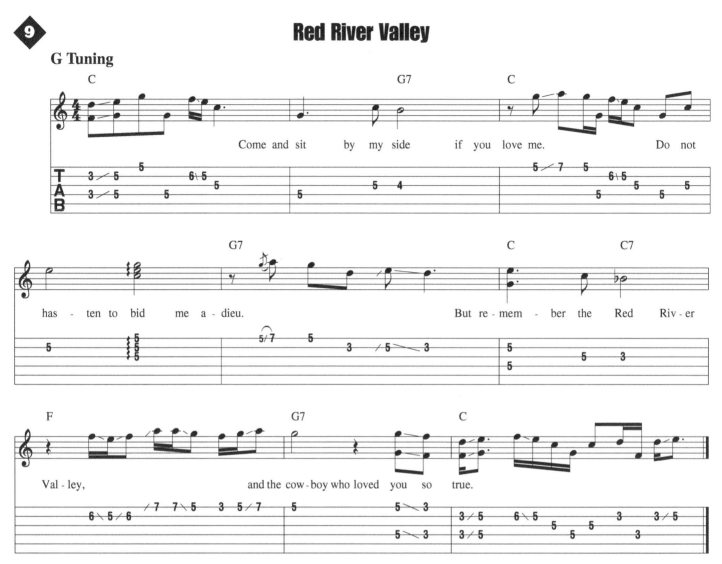

SUMMING UP — NOW YOU KNOW...

▶ *How to play a moveable blues scale in G tuning*

▶ *How to play a moveable major scale in G tuning*

▶ *How to use both scales to play melodies and ad lib solos and licks, in any key*

3

G TUNING: "FOLLOWING THE CHANGES"

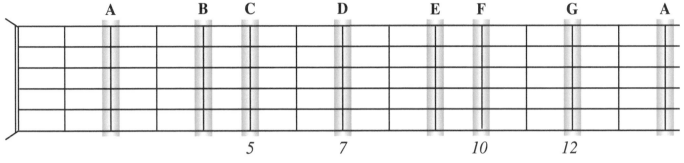

WHY?

▶ Instead of using *scales*, you can base solos and backup on chords, playing barred chords for every chord change in a tune.

WHAT?

▶ **ROADMAP #3** *shows all the barred major chords in G tuning.*

▶ *The sharp and flat major chords are between the indicated chords.* A barre at the 6th fret, one fret above C, is C♯ (D♭). A barre at the 8th fret, one fret below E, is E♭ (D♯).

▶ *The fretboard "starts over" at the 12th fret.* The G barre at the 12th fret matches the open string G chord; the 14th fret/A chord matches the 2nd fret/A, and so on.

HOW?

▶ *You can play chord-based licks and melodies by following a song's chord changes* and playing the appropriate barred chords.

▶ *Besides playing the notes of a barred chord, you can play major scale and blues scale notes* for each barre, like those described in **ROADMAP #2**.

▶ *The 1st string, five frets above a barre, is a high tonic note.* (The 1st string/10th fret, five frets above the C barre, is a high C note.) This "key note" is often useful in solos.

▶ *Harmonize the major scale by playing pairs of notes:* play the 5th and 3rd strings simultaneously, and the 4th and 2nd, 3rd and 2nd, and the 2nd and 1st:

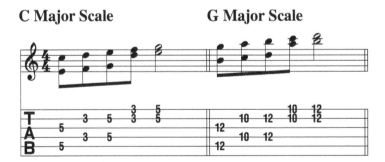

▶ *Before playing a song, make sure you know where the I, IV and V chords are. They are the three main chords in countless songs.*

▷ The I chord is the tonic (G, in the key of G).

15

▷ The IV chord is so named because its root is the 4th note of the major scale of the given key. C is the 4th note of the G major scale, so C (or C6, C7, etc.) is the IV chord in the key of G. The IV chord is always five frets above the I chord.

▷ The V chord is so named because its root is the 5th note of the major scale of the given key. It is always two frets above the IV chord (seven frets above the tonic).

Key of E:

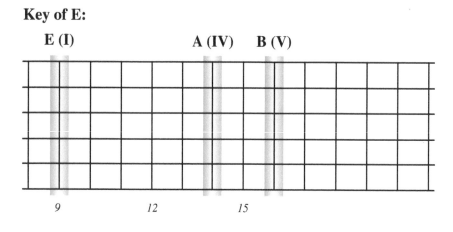

Key of C:

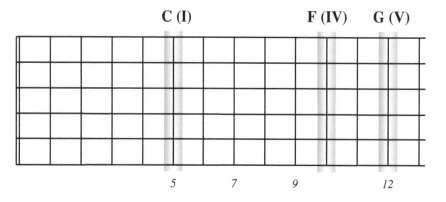

Key of A:

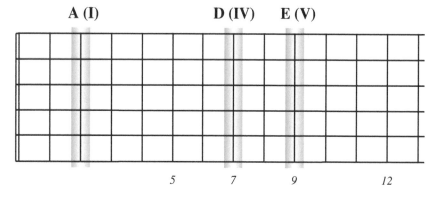

Key of F:

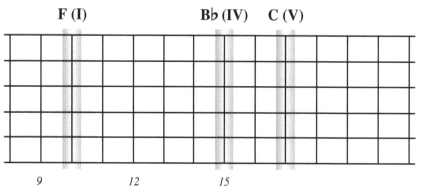

► *Find other chords (II, ♭VII, VI) by relating them to I, IV and V.* For example, the II chord is always two frets above the I chord. The ♭VII chord is always two frets below the I chord. The VI is two frets above the V.

DO IT!

► *Play backup and melody to "Stagolee" in the key of E, by following the song's chord changes:*

Stagolee

▶ *Play a chord-based solo and backup to "Sloop John B" in the key of F:*

Sloop John B.

G Tuning
Backup

Hoist up the John B. sails.   See how the main sails set.

Send for the cap-tain a- shore,   let me go home.   Let me go

home.   You know I wan-na go home.

feels so break up,   I wan-na go home.

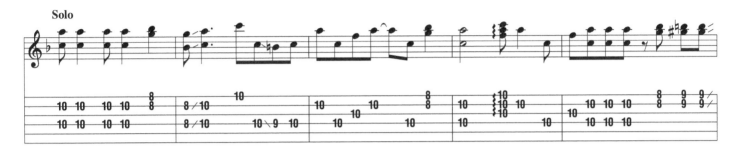

Solo

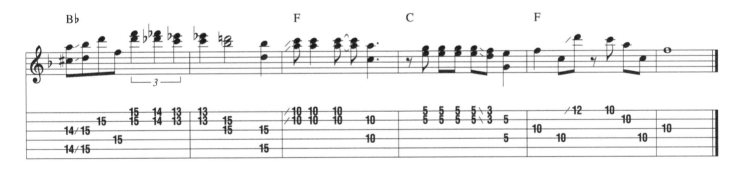

▶ *Here's a chord-based solo to the old country tune, "I Never Will Marry," in D:*

I Never Will Marry

12

G Tuning

▶ *This version of "Rocky Blues" is chord-based:*

Rocky Blues III (Chord-Based)

G Tuning

SUMMING UP—NOW YOU KNOW...

▶ *How to play all the barred major chords in G tuning*

▶ *How to play chord-based solos and backup in G tuning, in any key*

▶ *How to harmonizes licks and melodies by playing pairs of notes*

#4 G TUNING: MINOR CHORDS

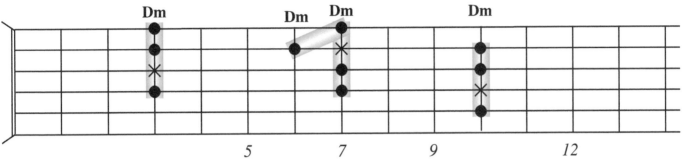

WHY?

▶ Many tunes include minor chords, and there are some tricks involved in playing them when your guitar is tuned to a major chord.

WHAT?

▶ *The above diagram shows several Dm chords.* They are actually two-note "partial chords."

▶ *The diagram shows how to find minor chords by relating them to the barred major chord.* For example, there's a Dm on the 1st and 2nd strings, *four frets below the barred D chord.* This is one way to find any minor chord: play the top two strings, four frets below a barred major chord.

▶ *There are two options for some of the positions.* For example, you can play a Dm on the 1st and 2nd strings/3rd fret, or on the 2nd and 4th strings/3rd fret.

HOW?

▶ *By simply not playing the 2nd or 5th strings, you can make any barred chord harmonize with a minor chord.* The resulting chord has no 3rd, so it's not major or minor, but it doesn't clash with a minor chord:

▶ *You can make any barred major chord into a minor chord by slanting back on the 2nd string.* It takes some practice to get the right intonation on slant chords, but it's worth the trouble. (See the illustration.)

► *You can make a barred chord minor by playing the 1st and 2nd strings (or 2nd and 4th strings) four frets below the barre:*

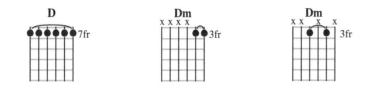

► There's another way to locate this minor chord: *it's one fret above its V chord.* In other words, to find a Dm, play the 1st and 2nd strings, one fret above the A barre, because A is a fifth above D. To play an Em, play the 1st and 2nd strings one fret above the B barre, as B is a fifth above E.

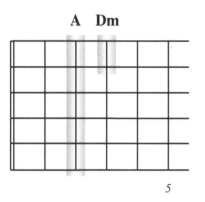

► *You can make a barred chord minor by playing the 2nd and 3rd (or 3rd and 5th) strings three frets above the barre:*

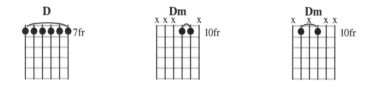

► A major chord is so frequently followed by its relative minor (the minor chord that is a 6th higher) that it is useful to have an automatic way to make this chord change. Here are two ways to find a relative minor chord:

▷ *You can play the relative minor to a barred chord by playing the 1st and 2nd strings (or 2nd and 4th strings) 5 frets above the barre:*

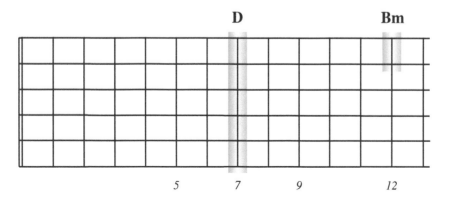

> *You can play the relative minor to a barred chord by playing the 1st and 3rd (or 3rd and 4th) strings 3 frets below the barre:*

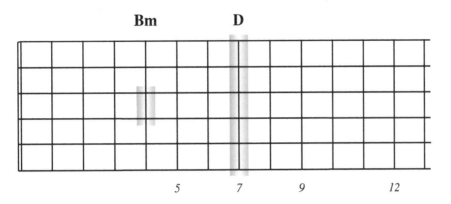

DO IT!

► The following songs include many minor chords. Before playing each tune, take stock of which minor chords are needed, and make sure you know a few positions for each one.

Wayfaring Stranger

G Tuning

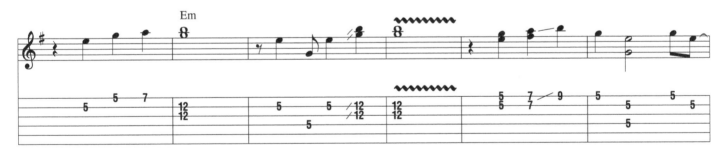

St. James Infirmary

G Tuning

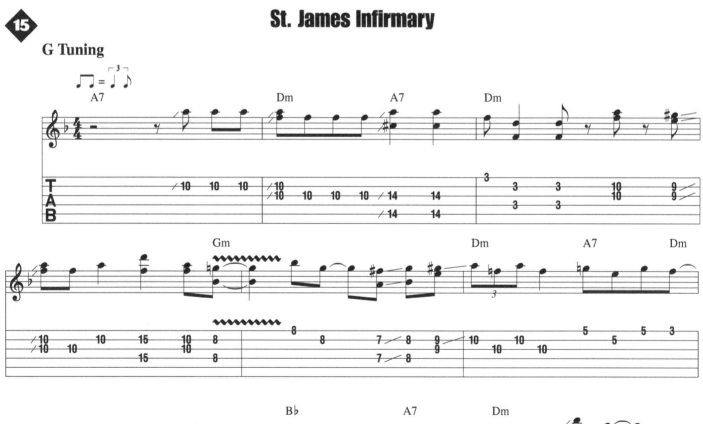

The Water Is Wide

G Tuning

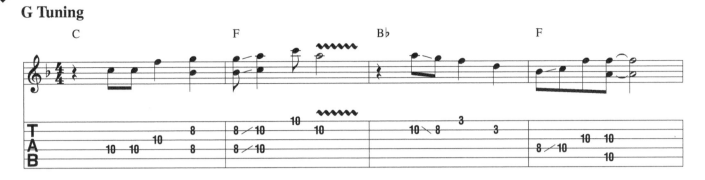

Scarborough Fair

G Tuning

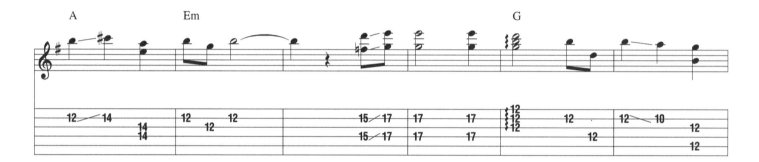

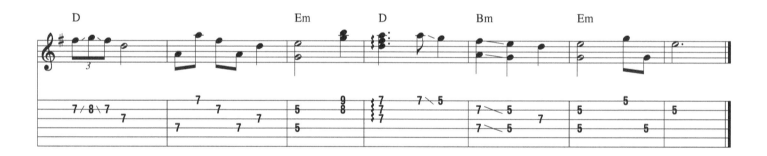

SUMMING UP—NOW YOU KNOW...

▶ *Several ways to play minor chords in G tuning*

▶ *How to find any major chord's relative minor*

G TUNING: MORE CHORDS

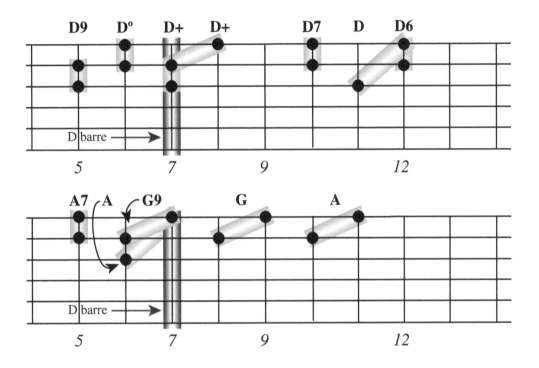

WHY?

▶ Here are some tips on how to improve your chord vocabulary. The ninth chords, sevenths and other chords pictured in **ROADMAP #5** add color to your playing and act as bridges to other chords.

WHAT?

▶ *The top diagram above shows how to play many D chords (D6, D7, D9, etc.).* Each new chord shape can be understood in terms of how it relates to the barred major chord. For example, the D7 is played on the 1st and 2nd (or 2nd and 4th) strings, three frets above the barred D chord.

▶ *The bottom diagram above shows how to find some IV and V chords (G9, A7, etc.) by relating them to the barred D major chord.*

▶ *The relationships on the above charts are moveable.* For example, you can turn any major chord into a seventh chord by playing the 1st and 2nd strings, three frets above the barre.

HOW?

▶ *7th chord: play the 1st and 2nd (or 2nd and 4th) strings, 3 frets above the barre.*

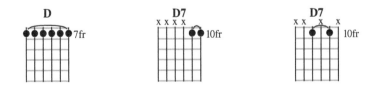

► *9th chord: play the 2nd and 3rd strings 2 frets below the barre.*

► *6th chord: play the 1st and 2nd (or 2nd and 4th) strings, 5 frets above the barre.*

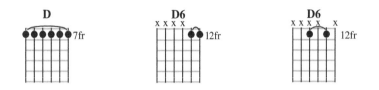

► *Diminished chord: play the 1st and 2nd (or 2nd and 4th) strings, 1 fret below the barre.* Since diminished chords repeat every 3 frets, you can play the same chord shape up or down 3 frets, 6 frets or 9 frets. (Diminished chords are written two ways: Cdim, C°.)

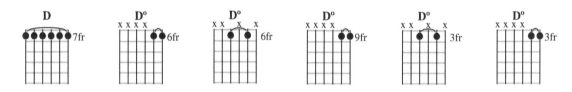

► *Augmented chord: play the 2nd and 3rd strings, at the barre*. Because augmented chords repeat every 4 frets, you can move this shape around, as you did the diminished chord shape, and you can play "whole step licks," as shown below. (Augmented chords are written two ways: Caug, C+.)

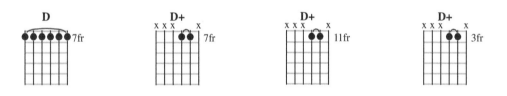

G Tuning

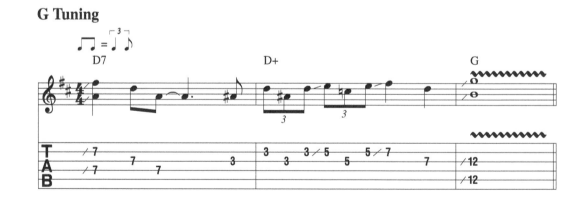

► You can also play an augmented chord by playing a slant on the 1st and 2nd strings at the barre:

▶ *Major chord with tonic (keynote) on the 1st string: play a slant chord on the 1st and 3rd strings, with the 1st string 5 frets above the barre.* In country music, this is often used in an ending lick:

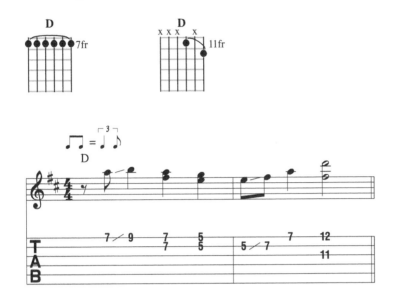

▶ *IV chord (major): play a slant chord on the 1st and 2nd strings, one fret above the barre.* You can move this chord up 2 frets to play the V chord.

▶ *IV chord (9th): play a slant on the 1st and 2nd strings, 1 fret below the barre.* You can move this chord up 2 frets the play the V chord.

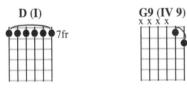

▶ *V chord (tonic on 1st string): play a slant on the 1st and 3rd strings, 1 fret below the barre.* You can move this shape down 2 frets to play the IV chord.

▶ *V chord (7th): play the 1st and 2nd (or 2nd and 4th) strings, 2 frets below the barre.* You can move this shape down 2 frets to play the IV chord.

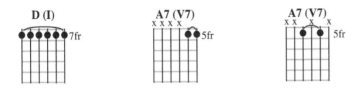

DO IT!

▶ The following backup and solos for two old folk blues make use of many of the above chord shapes. Notice how the 6ths and 9ths give "Corrinne, Corrinna" a swing sound. (Chords in parentheses are played by the steel guitar, not by the rhythm guitar.)

Corrinne, Corrinna

20

G Tuning
Backup

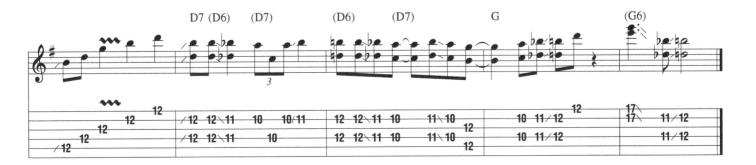

Tain't Nobody's Biz-niss

G Tuning
Backup

If I should take a no-tion to jump in-to the o-cean, it

Solo

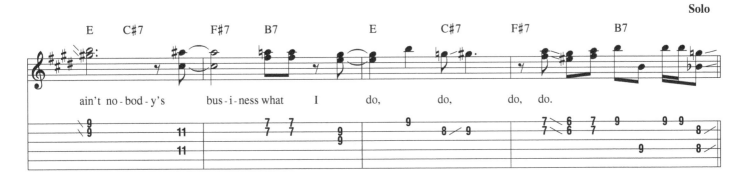

ain't no-bod-y's bus-i-ness what I do, do, do, do.

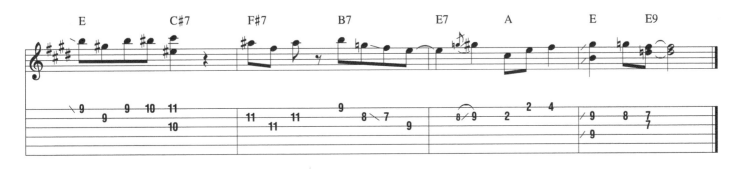

Turn Around

G Tuning

▶ This rock/ballad, which has a common pop progression, makes use of many chord shapes discussed in this chapter.

SUMMING UP—NOW YOU KNOW...

▶ *How to play 6ths, 7ths, 9ths, diminished and augmented chords*

▶ *How to play several IV and V chords, relative to a barred major chord*

D TUNING: FIRST POSITION

Blues Scale

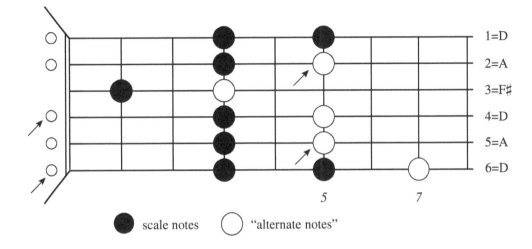

● scale notes   ○ "alternate notes"

Major Scale

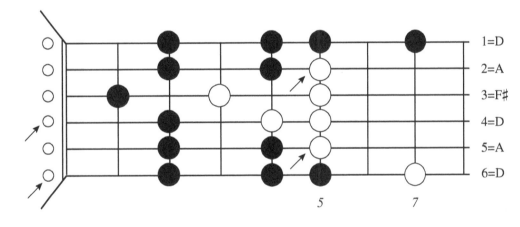

WHY?

▶ This popular open tuning has been used by blues, country and rock players.

WHAT?

▶ *The diagrams of* ROADMAP #6 *show the first position major and blues scales for open D tuning.* When you strum the open strings in this tuning, you play a D major chord.

▶ *The scales are guidelines.* Sometimes other notes (between the notes indicated above) work.

▶ *The arrows point out the tonic (D) notes.* In this tuning, there's an open high tonic note (D) on the 1st string.

▶ *The white dots are "alternates."* They are duplicated by open strings or by higher strings. For example, the 2nd string/5th fret and the open 1st string are both D. The 4th string/5th fret and the 3rd string/1st fret are both G.

HOW?

▶ *To get to D tuning from standard tuning:*

The 5th (A) and 4th (D) strings stay as they are in standard tuning.
Tune the 6th/E string down two frets, to D. Match it to the open 4th string.
Tune the 3rd/G string down one fret, to F♯. Match it to the 4th string/4th fret.

Tune the 2nd string down two frets, to A. Match it to the open 5th string.

Tune the 1st/E string down two frets, to D. Match it to the open 4th string.

▶ *Play the scales ascending and descending.*

D Tuning
D Blues Scale

D Tuning
D Major Scale

DO IT!

▶ *Use the blues scale to ad lib solos throughout a bluesy tune.* Here's "Blues Traveler" in the key of D, in D tuning. All the soloing is based on the D blues scale.

24

Blues Traveler

D Tuning

▶ *Use the blues scale to play melody and blues licks.* In the following solo, the guitar plays the melody and fills to "See, See Rider" in D tuning/key of D.

See, See Rider III (D Tuning)

D Tuning

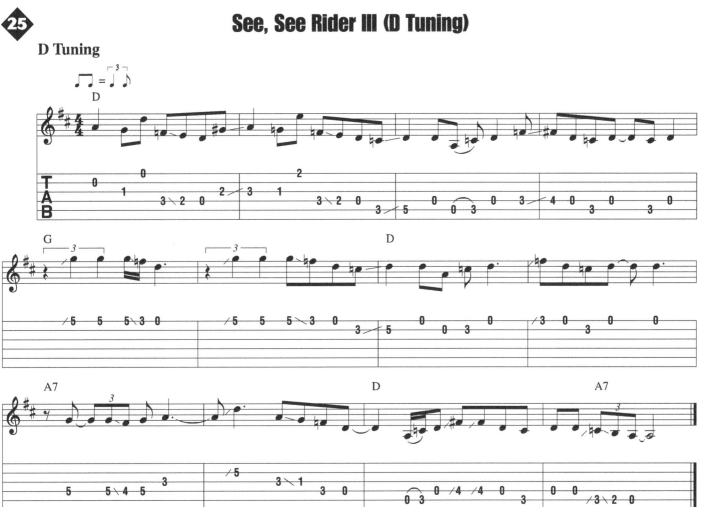

▶ *Use the major scale to play melodies and ad lib solos.* In "Streets of Laredo," below, the melody and fills that follow are based on the major scale.

Streets of Laredo

D Tuning

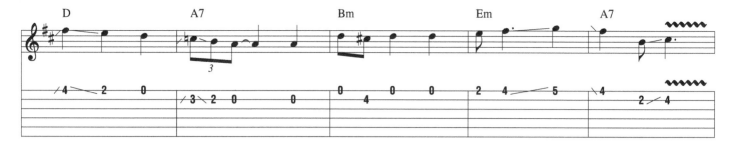

SUMMING UP—NOW YOU KNOW…

▶ *How to play a first-position D blues scale*

▶ *How to play a first-position D major scale*

▶ *How to use both scales to play melodies and ad lib solos and licks*

#7 THE G/D CONVERSION

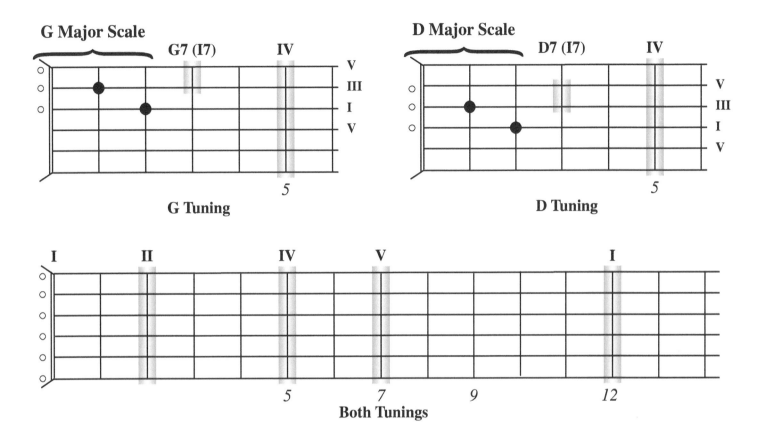

G Major Scale

G7 (I7) IV

G Tuning

D Major Scale

D7 (I7) IV

D Tuning

I II IV V I

5 7 9 12

Both Tunings

WHY?

▶ There's a relationship between the G and D tunings that makes it possible for you to borrow licks or solos from one tuning and use them in the other.

WHAT?

▶ *In D tuning, you can use G licks, scales, solos and chords if you "move them down a string."* A G tuning lick that is played on the 1st string can be played in D tuning on the 2nd string. A melody played on the 2nd and 3rd strings in G tuning can be played on the 3rd and 4th strings in D tuning. That's because the G tuning/string-to-string intervals on the top four strings (1st, 2nd, 3rd and 4th) match the D tuning/string-to-string intervals on the middle four strings (2nd, 3rd, 4th and 5th).

G TUNING INTERVALS	D TUNING INTERVALS
1st string = V	V = 2nd string
2nd string = III	III = 3rd string
3rd string = I	I = 4th string
4th string = V	V = 5th string

▶ *Conversely, you can steal many D tuning licks, scales, solos and chords and use them in G tuning by "moving them up a string."* Any D tuning lick or chord that doesn't use the 1st string is eligible for this conversion.

HOW?

▶ **When in D tuning, "convert" a G tuning lick by playing 1st string notes on the 2nd string, 2nd string notes on the 3rd string, and so on.** Here's a G tuning "turnaround" converted to D tuning. Note that chords, as well as licks, are "moved down a string." (A turnaround is a lick that ends an 8- or 12-bar phrase in a blues tune.)

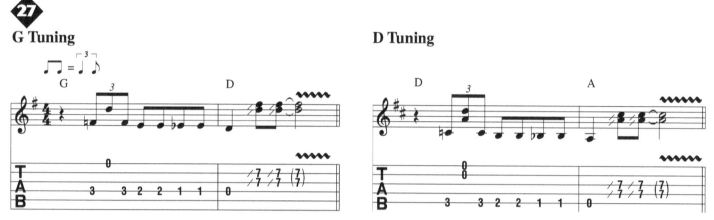

▶ **When in G tuning, "convert" a D tuning lick by playing it "one string higher,"** as this turnaround illustrates:

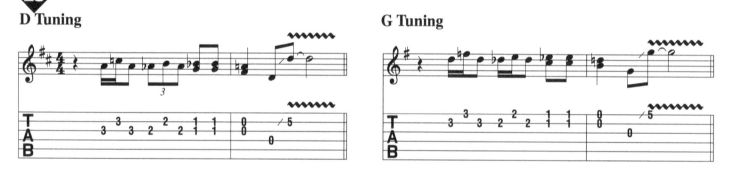

DO IT!

▶ *Here's "Chilly Winds" in D tuning, transposed from the G tuning version in the* ROADMAP *#1 chapter.* It's the exact same solo as in that chapter, moved down a string.

Chilly Winds II (D Tuning)

D Tuning

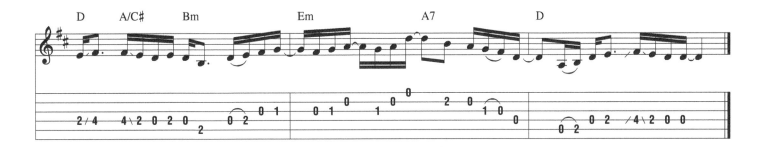

▶ *Here's "Streets of Laredo" in G tuning, transposed from the D tuning version in the* **ROADMAP #6** *chapter.* It's moved up a string from the G arrangement, and the second half of the tune, which was played mostly on the 1st string in D tuning, is not transposed.

Streets of Laredo II (G Tuning)

G Tuning

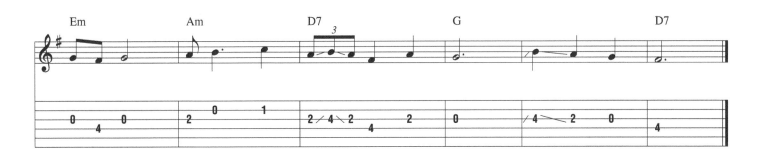

SUMMING UP—NOW YOU KNOW...

▶ *How to convert G tuning licks and solos to D tuning*

▶ *How to convert D tuning licks and solos to G tuning*

8

D TUNING: MOVEABLE SCALES

D Blues Scale **D Major Scale**

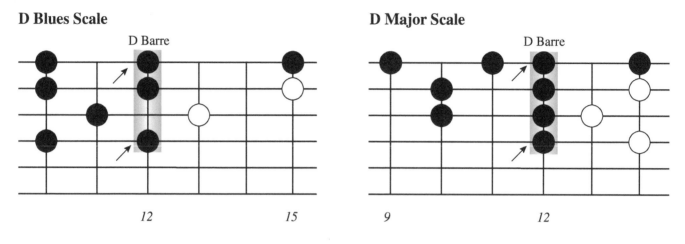

WHY?

▶ The scales in **ROADMAP #8** make it possible to solo and ad lib licks in any key, in D tuning.

WHAT?

▶ *The above diagrams show two moveable scales: D major and D blues.* Both scales have the same "home base": the barred D chord at the 12th fret. The arrows point out the tonic (D) notes.

▶ *The "inside 4 strings" (5, 4, 3 and 2) have the same scale configurations as the "top 4 strings" (4, 3, 2 and 1) in G tuning.* Therefore, you know most of the D tuning moveable scales already.

HOW?

▶ *Play the scales ascending and descending.*

D Tuning **D Tuning**
D Blues Scale **D Major Scale**

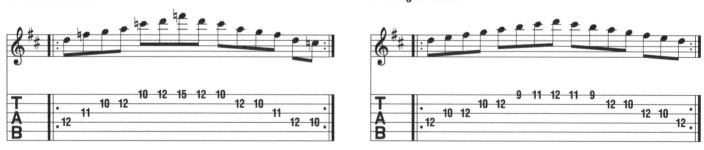

▶ *Play both moveable scales in other keys. Study the barre chord chart, below,* then play an A major scale, a C blues scale, etc.

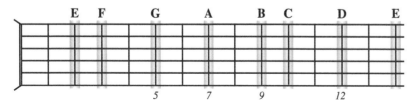

D Tuning
C Blues Scale

DO IT!

► *Use the moveable blues scale to ad lib solos to bluesy tunes* like "Elmore's Blues," which follows. It's a tip of the hat to the great Elmore James, who used this tuning.

Elmore's Blues

D Tuning

41

▶ *Use the moveable major scale to play melodies and solos in keys other than D.* Here's a melodic solo to "Amazing Grace" in the key of C (10th fret). It's very similar to the G tuning version in the **ROADMAP #2** chapter:

Amazing Grace II (D Tuning)

D Tuning

▶ *Use the moveable major scale to ad lib backup licks to "Careless Love"* in the key of E (14th fret):

Careless Love

D Tuning
Backup

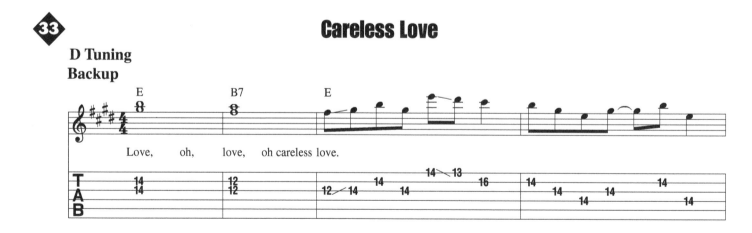

Love,   oh,   love,   oh careless love.

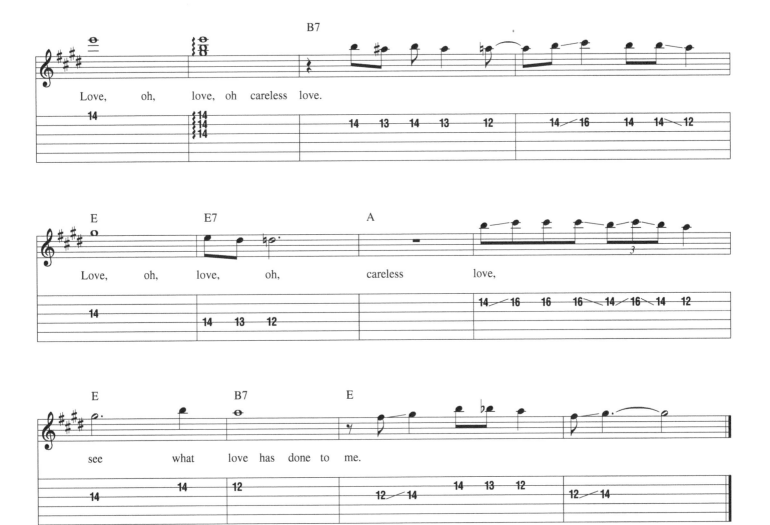

SUMMING UP—NOW YOU KNOW...

▶ *How to play a moveable blues scale in D tuning*

▶ *How to play a moveable major scale in D tuning*

▶ *How to use both scales to play melodies and ad lib solos and licks, in any key*

9

D TUNING: "FOLLOWING THE CHANGES"

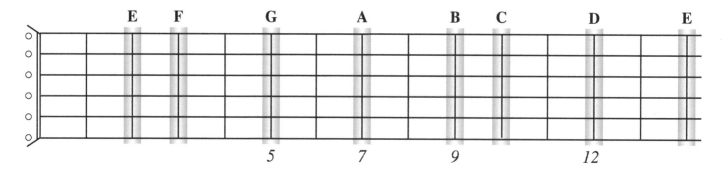

WHY?

▶ In D tuning, you can base solos and backup on chords, just as you did in G tuning.

WHAT?

▶ **ROADMAP #9** *shows all the barred major chords in D tuning.*

▶ *The sharp and flat major chords are between the indicated chords.* A barre at the 6th fret, one fret above G, is G♯ (A♭). A barre at the 8th fret, one fret below B, is B♭ (A♯).

▶ *The fretboard "starts over" at the 12th fret.* The D barre at the 12th fret matches the open string D chord; the 14th fret/E chord matches the 2nd fret/E.

HOW?

▶ *You can play chord-based licks and melodies by following a song's chord changes,* playing the appropriate barred chords.

▶ *Besides playing the notes of a barred chord, you can play major scale and blues scale notes for each barre,* like those described in the **ROADMAP #8** chapter.

▶ *Before playing a song, make sure you know where the I, IV and V chords are. They have the same relationships on the fretboard as in G tuning.*

▷ The IV chord is always five frets above the I chord.

▷ The V chord is always two frets above the IV chord (seven frets above the tonic) or five frets *below* the I chord.

Key of E:

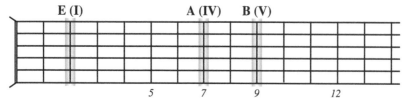

Key of C:

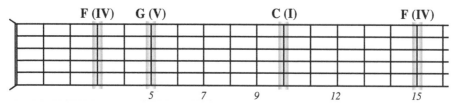

► ***Find other chords (II, ♭VII, VI) by relating them to I, IV and V.*** The II chord is always two frets above the I chord, the ♭VII chord is always two frets below the I chord, and so on.

DO IT!

► ***Play backup and melody to "Stagolee" in the key of E, by following the song's chord changes:***

Stagolee II (D Tuning)

34

D Tuning
Backup

45

> ► *You can play the 2nd and 3rd notes of the major scale on the 1st string, above the barre.* These notes will come in handy in countless tunes. For example, "Stagolee II," above, could have begun like this:

35

D Tuning

> ► *Here's a chord-based solo to "I Never Will Marry," in the key of G, in D tuning:*

36

I Never Will Marry II (D Tuning)

D Tuning

▶ *The solo to "Southern Rock," in the key of A, is chord-based:*

Southern Rock

D Tuning

SUMMING UP—NOW YOU KNOW...

▶ *How to play all the barred major chords in D tuning*

▶ *How to play chord-based solos and backup in D tuning, in any key*

10

D TUNING: CHORDS AND THE G/D CONVERSION

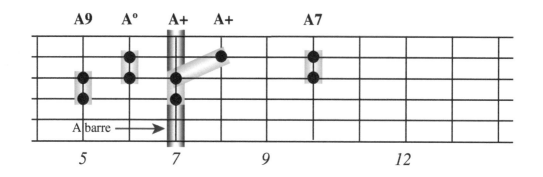

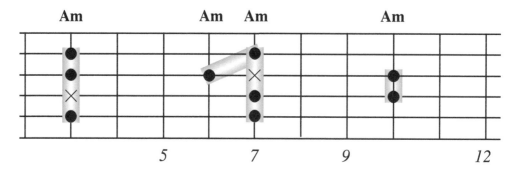

WHY?

▶ You can acquire a large chord vocabulary in D tuning by taking the chord ideas of **ROADMAPS #4** and **#5** and "moving them up a string."

WHAT?

▶ *The above diagrams show how to find many A chords (A7, A9, etc.) by relating them to the barred A chord.* For example, there's an A7 on the 2nd and 3rd strings, three frets above the barred A chord.

▶ **ROADMAP #10** *shows moveable chord relationships.* For example, to play any 7th chord in D tuning, play the 2nd and 3rd strings, three frets above the barred major chord.

▶ *All the chord shapes of* **ROADMAP #10** *are "moved up a string" from the G tuning chords.* In G tuning, to play a 9th chord, you play the 2nd and 3rd strings two frets below a barred major chord. In D tuning, to play a 9th chord, you play the 3rd and 4th strings two frets below the barred major chord.

HOW?

▶ *Here are some examples of G tuning to D tuning chord conversions.* You can convert all the chords in Chapters 4 and 5 in a similar fashion:

▷ *You can make any barred major chord into a minor chord by slanting back on the 3rd string.*

▷ *7th chord: play the 2nd and 3rd (or 3rd and 5th) strings, 3 frets above the barre.*

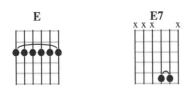

▷ *9th chord: play the 3rd and 4th strings 2 frets below the barre.*

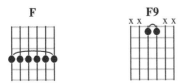

▷ *Diminished chord: play the 2nd and 3rd (or 3rd and 5th) strings, 1 fret below the barre.*

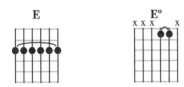

DO IT!

▶ Play the following tunes, converted to D tuning from the G tuning versions in previous chapters:

Wayfaring Stranger II (D Tuning)

D Tuning

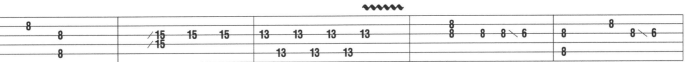

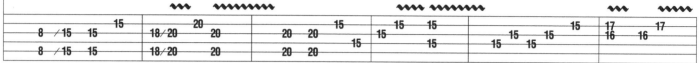

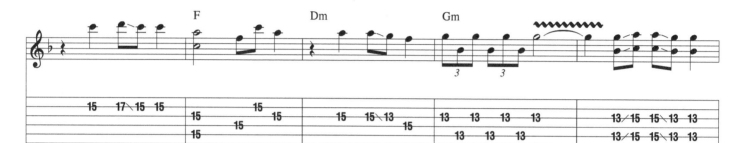

Turn Around II (D Tuning)

SUMMING UP—NOW YOU KNOW...

► *How to play minor chords, 9ths, 7ths, 6ths, diminished and augmented chords by converting G tuning chord shapes to D tuning*

11

THE G/A AND D/E CONVERSION

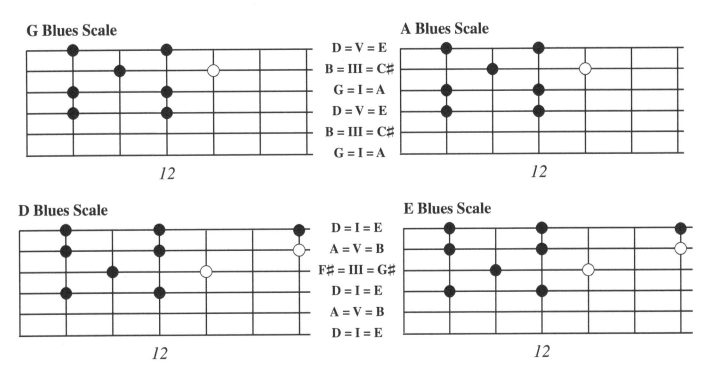

G Blues Scale

D = V = E
B = III = C#
G = I = A
D = V = E
B = III = C#
G = I = A

A Blues Scale

12

D Blues Scale

D = I = E
A = V = B
F# = III = G#
D = I = E
A = V = B
D = I = E

E Blues Scale

12

WHY?

▶ Many lap-style players tune to the key of the song they're playing, because they like to have an open tonic chord. For example, to play a tune in F they tune to an open F chord. You can use the G or D tunings as a basis for any open chord.

WHAT?

▶ *"Open A" tuning is the same as G tuning, with every string tuned 2 frets (a whole step) higher.*

▶ *"Open E" tuning is the same as D tuning, with every string tuned 2 frets higher.*

▶ *"Open F" tuning is the same as G tuning, with every string tuned 2 frets lower; or you can use D tuning, with every string tuned 3 frets higher.*

▶ *You can tune to any open chord this way:*

Ab = G tuning 1 fret up	C# = D tuning 1 fret down
A = G tuning 2 frets up	Eb = D tuning 1 fret up
Bb = G tuning 3 frets up	E = D tuning 2 frets up
B = G tuning 4 frets up or D tuning 3 frets down	F = D tuning 3 frets up or G tuning 2 frets down
C = D tuning 2 frets down	Gb = G tuning 1 fret down

HOW?

► *When you play in any of these "converted" tunings, the chord shapes and relationships remain the same as in the tuning from which you converted, but the chord names change.*

▷ In open A tuning, all the G tuning chords and licks apply, but all the names of chords are a whole step (2 frets) higher, because A is a whole step above G.

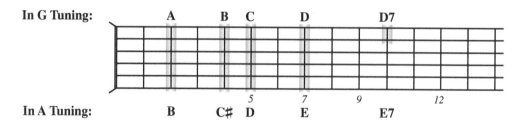

▷ In open C tuning, the D tuning chords and licks apply, but all the names of chords are a whole step (2 frets) lower, because C is a whole step below D.

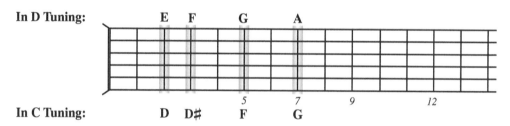

DO IT!

► Try playing some of the tunes in previous chapters in alternate tunings. Play the **ROADMAP #1** arrangement of "See See Rider" in open A (instead of open G), or **ROADMAP #8**'s "Elmore's Blues" in E tuning (instead of D).

SUMMING UP—NOW YOU KNOW...

► *How to tune to any open chord*

► *How to play steel licks and solos in any key, with an open tonic chord*

#12 HARMONICS

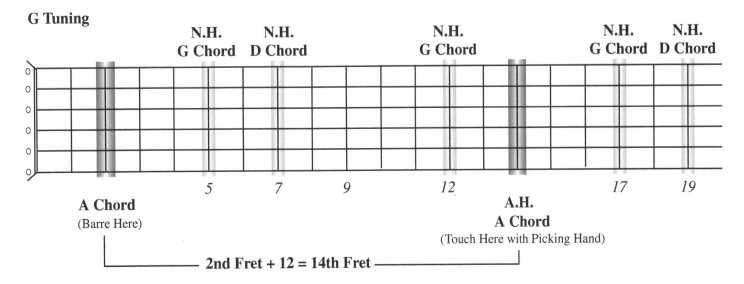

G Tuning

N.H. G Chord   N.H. D Chord   N.H. G Chord   N.H. G Chord   N.H. D Chord

5   7   9   12   17   19

A Chord
(Barre Here)

A.H.
A Chord
(Touch Here with Picking Hand)

2nd Fret + 12 = 14th Fret

WHY?

▶ Harmonics add color and variety to solos and backup. Dobro and steel players have been using them since the earliest recordings of lap guitars.

WHAT?

▶ *Harmonics are the bell-like notes you get by lightly touching the strings at certain strategic places while picking them.* **ROADMAP #12** shows where to touch the strings for harmonics.

▶ *"Natural harmonics" are played by touching or barring strings with your fretting hand* at the places marked "N.H." in Roadmap #12. There are other places to play natural harmonics, but these are the easiest spots.

▶ *"Artificial harmonics" are played by touching or barring strings with the picking hand,* as in the sample A chord that is marked "A.H." in **ROADMAP #12**.

▶ *Natural harmonics only can be played certain places on the fretboard, but any note can be played with artificial harmonics.*

HOW?

▶ *To play natural harmonics, touch the strings lightly with the side of the little finger of your fretting hand, as shown in this photo:*

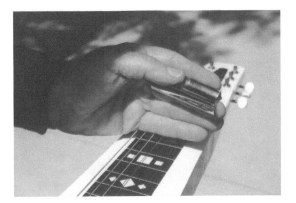

▷ Pick the strings as usual, once they are "fretted" at the right place.

▷ Instantly remove your fretting hand from the strings after picking them, or the sound will be muted.

▷ To get a clear, bell-like chime, touch the strings very lightly *right* over the fret markings.

40

G Tuning

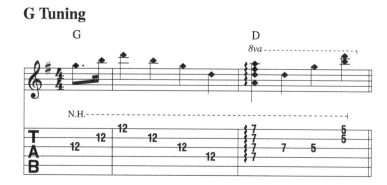

▷ Notice that the two D chords in the **ROADMAPS #12** chart sound the same, but the G chord at the 5th fret is an octave higher than the G chord at the 12th fret.

▷ *In D tuning, as in G tuning, the 5th and 12th frets give you natural harmonics for a I chord; the 7th and 19th frets give you natural harmonics for a V chord.* (In the key of D, the I chord is D and the V chord is A.)

▶ *To play artificial harmonics:*

▷ Fret two or three strings as usual, with the steel.

▷ Touch the strings 12 frets above the fret point, with the side of your picking hand, as shown in *Photo #1,* below.

▷ Pick the strings with the thumb of your picking hand.

▷ Immediately remove the side of your hand from the strings after picking them, so they will not be muted.

▷ Play an artificial harmonic on a single string by "fretting" it with the ring finger of your picking hand, and picking it with your thumb (which is curled under the ring finger) as shown in *Photo #2,* below:

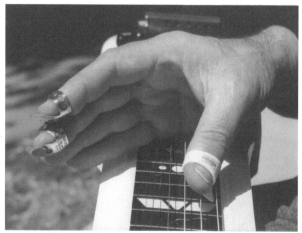

Photo #1: Playing a chord with artificial harmonics

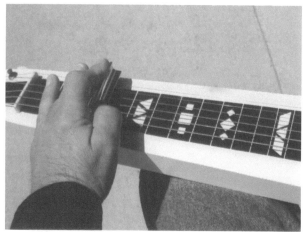

Photo #2: Playing a single string with artificial harmonics

G Tuning

DO IT!

▶ Play "Chimes," below, an instrumental that features artificial and natural harmonics.

Chimes

G Tuning

SUMMING UP—NOW YOU KNOW…

▶ *How to play certain chords or single notes with natural harmonics*

▶ *How to play any chord or single note with artificial harmonics*

USING THE PRACTICE TRACKS

On the four practice tracks, the lap-slide guitar is separated from the rest of the band— it's on just one side of the stereo image of your media player. You can tune it out and use the band as backup, trying out any soloing techniques you like. You can also imitate the lead guitar; here are the soloing ideas on each track:

TRACK #1: 12-BAR BLUES/ROCK IN G and D (G Tuning)

43 ▶ This one goes four times around a 12-bar blues. The F chord in the 9th bar is a slight variation of the usual progression.

▷ During the 1st 12 bars, the solo consists of first position G blues licks.

▷ In the 2nd 12 bars, the solo consists of moveable G blues licks at the 12th fret.

▷ The 3rd 12 bars, the solo follows the chord changes, with licks based on each barred chord.

▷ The 4th time, the tune modulates to the key of D. The solo follows the tune's chord changes, with licks based on the various barred chords.

TRACK #2: "THE WATER IS WIDE" in D (G Tuning)

44 ▶ Playing twice around this 16-bar tune, the soloist offers many examples of how to deal with minor chords. Here's the progression:

| D | G | D | ╱. | Bm | ╱. | Em | A7 |
| F#m | ╱. | Bm | G | D | A | D | ╱. |

TRACK #3: 8-BAR BLUES SHUFFLE IN D and E (D Tuning)

45 ▶ The solos follow the same pattern as #1:

▷ 8 bars of first position D blues licks

▷ 8 bars of moveable D blues licks at the 12th fret

▷ 8 bars of moveable licks based on barred chords, using a barred chord for each chord change

▷ 8 bars of moveable licks based on barred chords, in the key of E

Here's the basic progression in D:

| D7 | ╱. | G7 | ╱. | D7 | A7 | D7 | A7 |

TRACK #4: COUNTRY/ROCK TUNE IN C (D Tuning)

46 ▶ There are two 8-bar sections to this tune, each played twice in a row. The soloist goes twice around the whole thirty-two bars, playing chord-based licks:

| ‖: C | ╱. | Am | ╱. | C | ╱. | D7 | G :‖ |
| ‖: F | F#° | C/G | A | F | F#° | C/G | G7 :‖ |